Broken Shells

let adversity create beauty in you

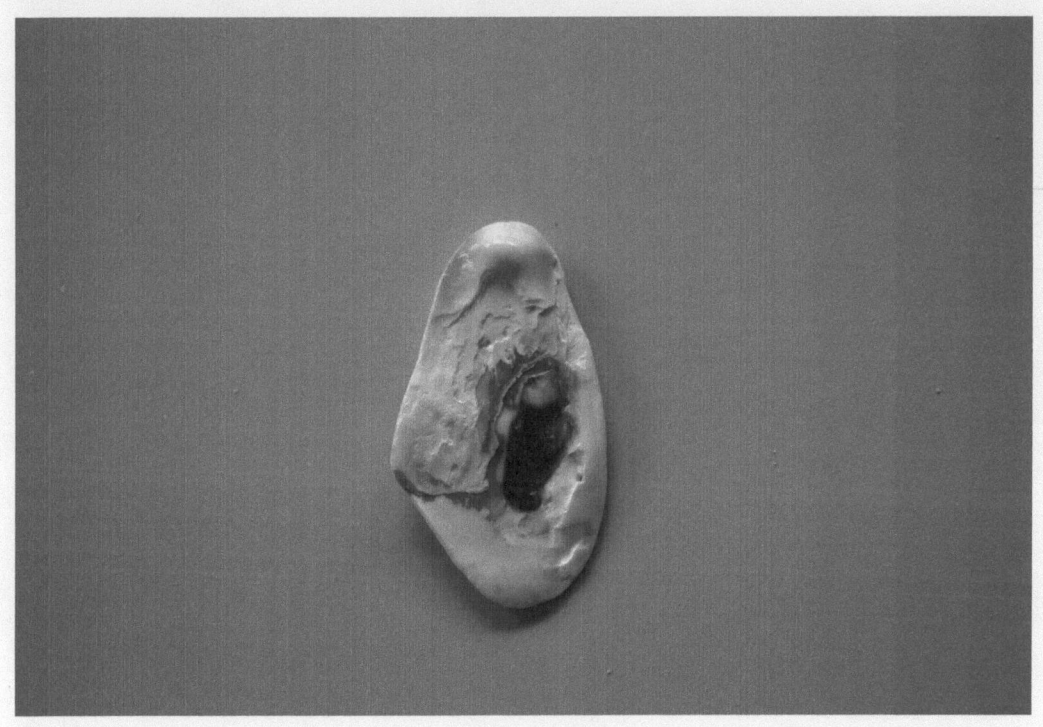

elizabeth curcio

This book is dedicated to God and my family and friends who are my helpers and cheerleaders. Without them, this book would not be possible.

As I was walking along the shore one day, I asked God if I could find a pearl in a shell.

Instead, He gave me words of wisdom and broken shells.

When you are broken, a mosaic I can use.

Your adversities are My universities.

Think of your weaknesses as gifts.

I love finding shells but I rarely find one that is not broken. So I started looking for broken shells and found many. Broken shells worn down by adversity, pounded by waves and weather; rounded edges and beautiful.

Let adversity create beauty in you.

Elizabeth Curcio 2009 C

...My grace is sufficient for thee, for my strength is made perfect in weakness... 2 Cor. 12:9

No mention shall be made of coral, or of pearls, for the price of wisdom is above rubies. Job 28:18

angel's wing, wise man, Mary and baby Jesus, moon

vest, sweater, ballet shoes, tie

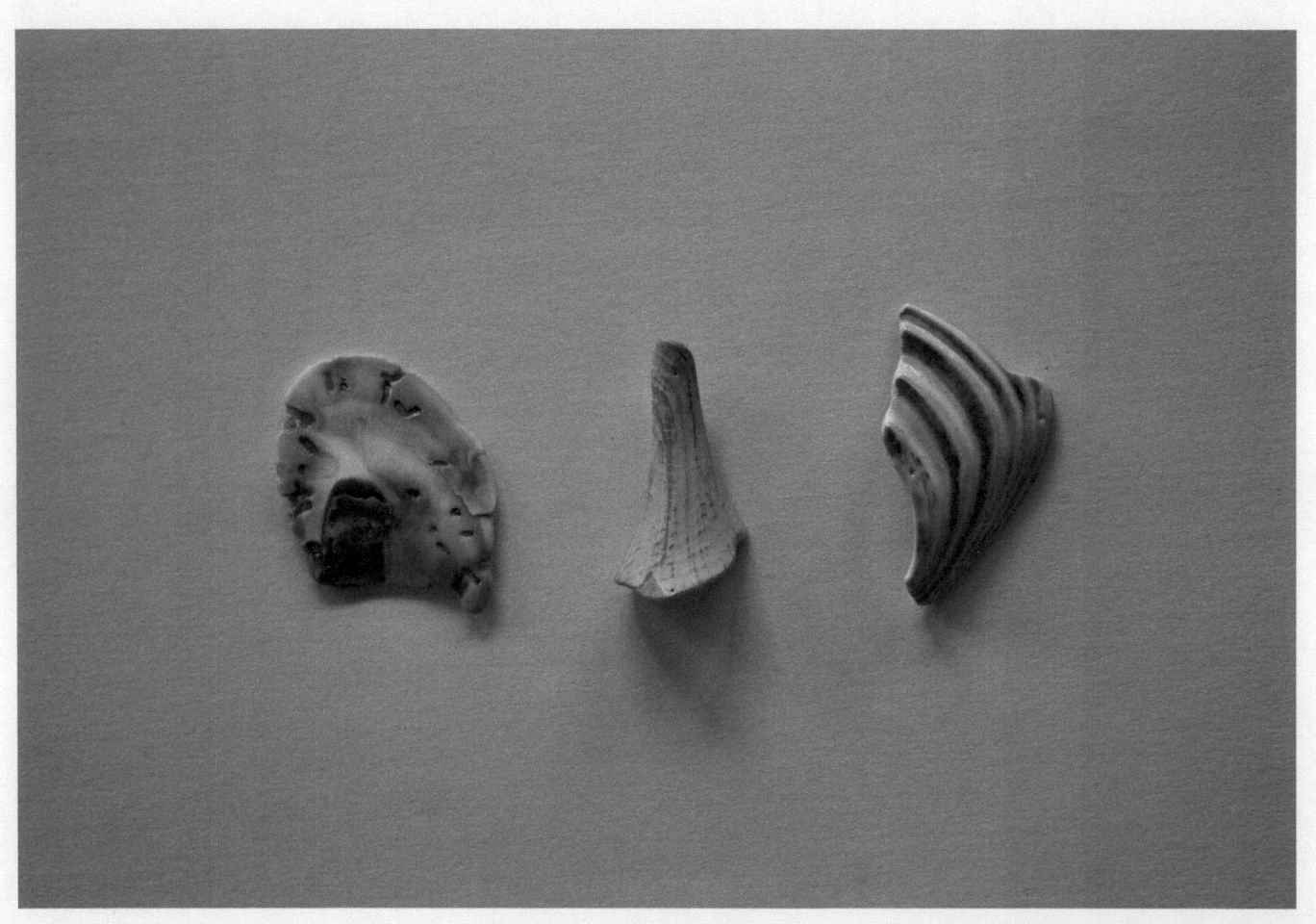

English cottage, Eiffel shell, fleur-de-lis

lightning, man in the moon, UFO, galaxy

marshmallow, blueberry pie, American flag, pizza

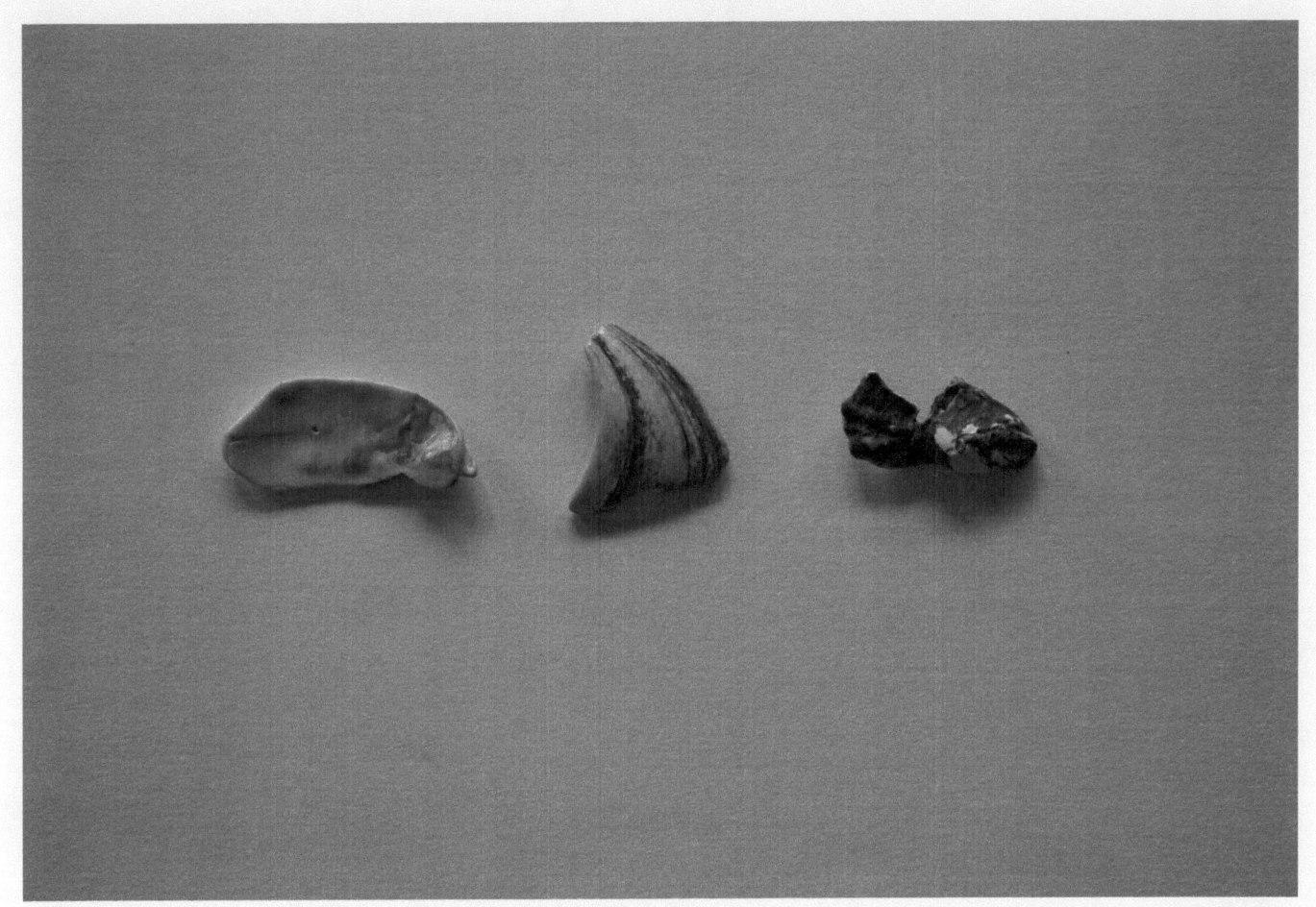

fish

more fish

bunny, squirrel, hedgehog

seagulls and surf

core, winter trees, glaciers

pumpkin, mushroom, key, baseball mitt

day at the salon, super cave guy, springtime

driftwood, stingray, fish

bird, lion cub, gorilla

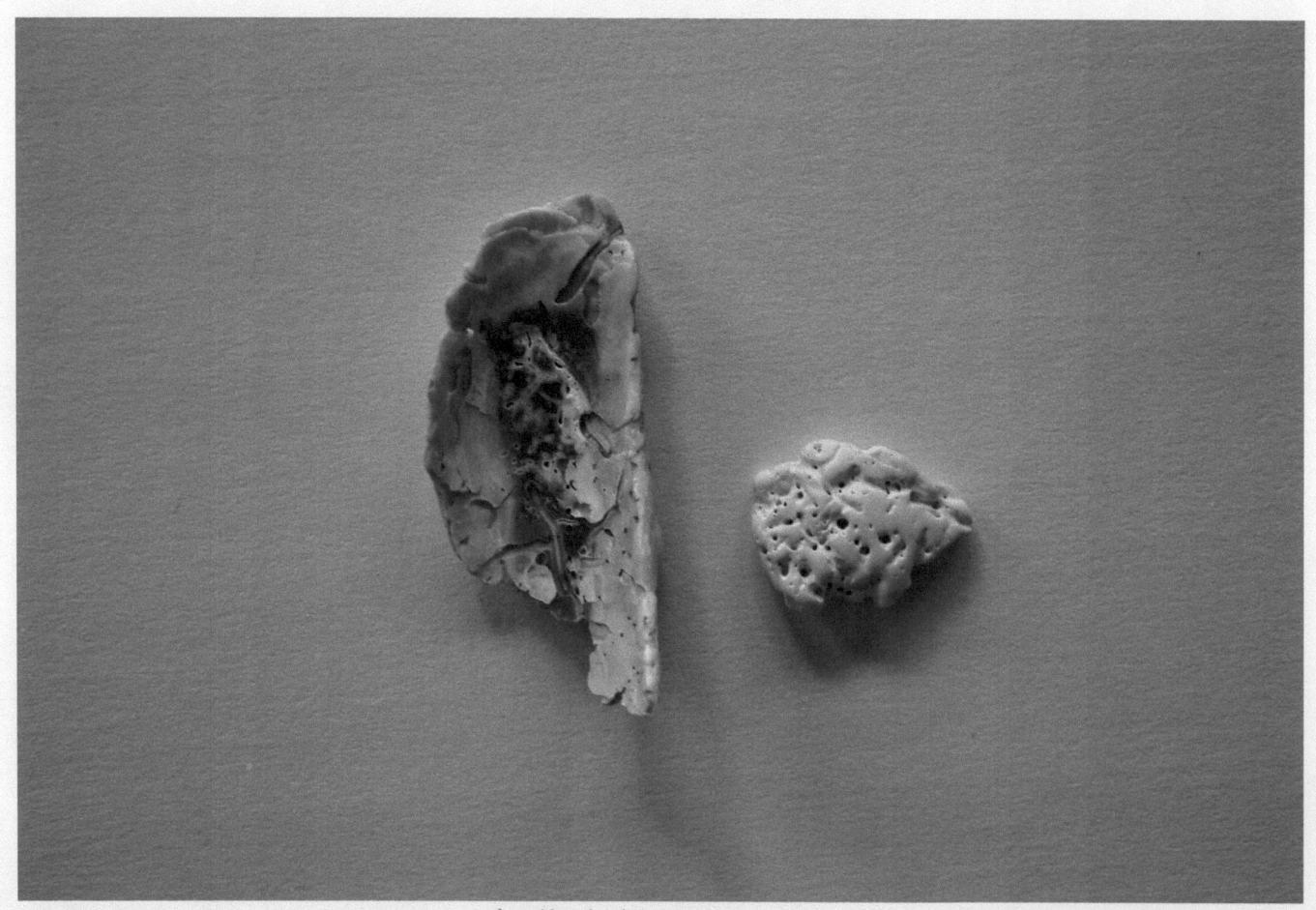

giraffe, baby stegosaurus

ark

hat, visors, layer cake

famous movie character   -   guess!